Loving People Who Are Hard to Love

Study Guide

**Transforming Your World by
Learning to Love Unconditionally**

JOYCE MEYER

FaithWords

NEW YORK · NASHVILLE

T0017813

FaithWords
Hachette Book Group
1290 Avenue of the Americas, New York, NY 10104
faithwords.com
twitter.com/faithwords

First Edition: September 2022

FaithWords is a division of Hachette Book Group, Inc.
The FaithWords name and logo are trademarks of Hachette Book Group, Inc.

The publisher is not responsible for websites (or their content) that are not owned by the
publisher.

The Hachette Speakers Bureau provides a wide range of authors for speaking events.
To find out more, go to www.hachettespeakersbureau.com or call (866) 376-6591.

The author would like to thank Beth Clark for her excellent editorial work on this project.

ISBN: 978-1-5460-1611-3

Printed in the United States of America

LSC-C

Printing 1, 2022

CONTENTS

INTRODUCTION

Let's face it. Some people in our lives are easier to love than others. When you think about those who are easy to love and those who are difficult to love, several names and faces probably come to mind right away. You know who poses a challenge to you when you think about loving them. Learning to love the ones who are hard to love is a process. I will admit it's not the most fun thing you will ever do, but it is an act of obedience to God's Word, and therefore it will bring great blessing into your life.

I wrote the book *Loving People Who Are Hard to Love* because I believe there is too much division, anger, hatred, and ill will in the world today, and the way to change that is for one person at a time to love those who are difficult to love. The world can become a better place one relationship at a time, and as you learn to love as God loves, you can be part of that transformation. Loving those who are hard to love will not only benefit the world, but it will also bring greater peace, satisfaction, and joy to your personal life. Remember, love is not a feeling; it's how we treat people.

The purpose of this study guide is to help you apply in practical ways the teachings of the book *Loving People Who Are Hard to Love*. As I mentioned in the introduction to that book, unless we become really good at not being easily offended and extending forgiveness to those who hurt us, I don't think there is any hope for peace and unity in the world. We are not born knowing how to love and forgive, and our human nature tends to be offended instead of extending grace and love to people who mistreat us. This is why I say we need to *become* really good at not being easily offended and extending forgiveness. It doesn't happen unless we work on it, but it is possible. We can develop the habit of forgiving everyone who hurts us, train ourselves not to be quickly or easily offended, and develop the ability to love people who are hard to love.

I mention this in the book, but I want to call your attention to it again here, because I think it will encourage you.

> Years ago, when God showed me how selfish I was and I started trying to learn how to love people, I had to deliberately try to think about it all the time. Now that I have practiced love for years, I think about it without having to make much of an effort to do so. The same will happen to you. Anytime we form a habit, it is difficult at first. We do it and then we forget to do it, and after a while something happens and we remember again and do it for a while and then forget again. But if we don't give up and we continue praying and asking God for help, we will become more loving people.

In this study guide, you'll find the following features to help you love people who are hard to love:

- **Growing in Love:** These questions are designed to help you apply the teachings and principles in *Loving People Who Are Hard to Love* so you will be strengthened in your ability to love all people. They are closely tied to the material in the book, and they follow the progression of each chapter, so if you want to see what the book says, you should be able to find it easily.
- **Living and Loving by the Word:** We often hear about "living by the Word," but we also learn to love from the Word of God. These questions provide you with an opportunity to revisit many of the scriptures mentioned in the book so you can apply them to your life.

- **What Do You Think?:** Throughout the book, you read a lot about what I think regarding certain matters. "What Do You Think?" is a section that allows you to think through topics or situations for yourself and to consider how the teachings of the book relate to the personal situations you may be facing right now.
- **Take the Love Challenge:** One thing you see clearly in *Loving People Who Are Hard to Love* is that loving isn't easy. At the end of each chapter of this study guide, I invite you to "Take the Love Challenge" by choosing to do something specific that will help you grow in loving God, yourself, or other people.

I want to make an important point for those who may respond directly to some of the questions in this study guide by jotting down their answers in the book itself. Because of the subject matter, you might not want anyone to see some of your responses, especially the people you are writing about. By design, the study guide does ask you to think of people who are hard to love, but it does not ask you to list their names. So think about how you use this guide, and be careful where you leave it if you don't want the people in your household, workplace, or other places to possibly read something that would hurt your relationship with them.

I hope and pray that this study guide will help you take the next steps you need to take toward loving the people in your life who are hard to love, and that you will experience the rewards of doing so as you seek to obey Jesus' instruction:

> Love one another. As I have loved you, so you must love one another. By this everyone will know that you are my disciples, if you love one another.
>
> John 13:34–35

PART 1

Love Changes Everything

The Greatest Thing in All the World

Growing in Love

1. Fill in the blanks from this sentence in the third paragraph of chapter 1:

   "Love gives life _____ and _____."

2. Do you know anyone who seems to be looking for love in all kinds of places, except in God? Why will they never find love unless they seek it in Him? Take time today to pray for that person.

3. Up to this point, how has love (either given or received) brought meaning and purpose to your life?

4. God is love, and He cannot do anything but love, because love is His nature. How does this set us free from trying to earn His love?

5. What did you learn from the story of Martuin Avdyéitch?

6. Think of a time when you did something loving for someone and they received it as a blessing from the Lord. How did it affect the person, and how did it affect you?

7. Where does loving people fall on your list of priorities? In other words, how important is it to you?

8. Some people say they love you while their actions prove they do not love you at all. Have you encountered this? Ask God to help you clearly recognize when people truly love you and when they do not.

9. If someone has hurt you while telling you they love you, forgiving them may be difficult, but it will set you free from them. I urge you to choose to forgive them, even if you don't feel like it. You may even want to write it down: "Lord, I deliberately choose to forgive _____ on _____."

10. Love is a choice we make when we desire to obey God, and it can be difficult. Is there a difficult decision you believe God is asking you to make in order to express love to someone who has hurt you, even if you do not feel like showing love? What is it?

11. Fill in the blanks in this sentence from paragraph 5 of the section "What Love Is Not":

    "Love sees the _____ in people, and it is willing to _____ about and be _____ with the aspects of people that aren't so good."

12. How can you pray for and be patient with someone who frustrates or offends you?

13. Love believes the best about other people, even when they do things we do not like, approve of, or understand. How can you show love to someone today by believing the best, not the worst, about them?

14. Fill in the blanks in these sentences from paragraph 6 of the section "What Love Is Not":

    "Love is not _____ and _____, and it doesn't have to be right. As a matter of fact, love _____ its right to be right."

15. What does it mean to sacrifice your right to be right? In what specific situation could you put this into practice?

16. If you have not read *The Five Love Languages* by Gary Chapman, I recommend it as a helpful resource for growing in your ability to give and receive love. Chapman has identified five love languages, which are listed below and are self-explanatory. Put a number alongside each one, indicating how important it is to you. For example, if quality time is the most important to you, put a 1 next to it. If gifts are least important to you, put a 5. What can you learn about yourself through this simple exercise?
    - quality time
    - acts of service
    - words of affirmation
    - gifts
    - physical touch

17. Complete this sentence from the last paragraph of chapter 1:
    "Nothing gives people more joy than _____ _____."

18. How can you give someone joy today by showing them you love them in some specific way? Think about the following types of people:
    - A family member
    - A person at work
    - A neighbor
    - A store clerk, a mail carrier, a bank teller, a bus driver, a gate agent at the airport, or some other service provider
    - A stranger
    - An individual you don't particularly like
    - Someone who has hurt or wronged you

19. After reading chapter 1, how would you describe what love is and what love is not? Why is it the greatest thing in all the world?

Living and Loving by the Word

1. Fill in the blank from the opening scripture of the chapter, which is 1 Corinthians 13:13:

   "And now these three remain: _____, _____ and _____. But the greatest of these is _____."

2. First John 4:8 and 4:16 teach us that God is love. How can you grow in accepting the love God has for you because of who He is, not because of anything you do or don't do?

3. What does Romans 5:8 teach us about God's love and how He expresses it through the greatest sacrifice imaginable—the sacrifice of His Son? In what way does knowing that Jesus sacrificed Himself for us increase your willingness to love people even when they have sinned against you?

4. What can you learn about love from Paul's prayer for the early believers in Philippians 1:9 and from his writing in 1 Thessalonians 3:12?

5. Colossians 3:14 teaches us to "put on love." How can you do this intentionally today?

What Do You Think?

You have read why I think love is the greatest thing in all the world. Now, why do *you* think love is so great?

Take the Love Challenge

I challenge you today to make one simple commitment to God by saying, "Lord, I commit myself to being part of the change that is so needed in the world today by learning to love the people in my life who are hard to love. Teach me how to do this."

CHAPTER 2

Loving People Who Are Hard to Love

Growing in Love

1. In a grocery store, you may have seen dented cans with no labels. Like these cans, do you have dents that have affected your life or the way you relate to people? What is "unlabeled" or "dented" about you?

2. What are some of the dents or surprises you have encountered in people you find challenging to love?

3. What can you do to enjoy your life while you are dealing with someone who is difficult to love?

4. How would you define a "porcupine person"? In what ways have you been a porcupine person at times, and why do you think you behaved that way?

5. Fill in the blanks from this sentence in the last paragraph of the section "Porcupine People":

    "We may sustain little _____ from time to time as we walk through life with other people, but we are much better off in _____ than in _____."

6. Why are people better off in relationships than in isolation, even though we sometimes get hurt in relationships?

7. What decisions do you need to make to live in less isolation and in greater relationship with others?

8. Chapter 2 includes a section called "Practical Steps to Loving People Who Are Hard to Love." The questions below are based on those steps.

   • Have you assumed you can love people who are hard to love by simply *trying* to love them? Ask God today to give you grace and help as you endeavor to love them.

   • Are you praying for people you find difficult to love? If not, it's never too late to start. Think about the people you need to pray for, and ask God to do whatever He needs to do in their lives.

   • Are you being a good example as you live your life before people who are challenging to you? What old behaviors do you need to change, or what new ones do you need to develop in order to be a good example of God's love to them?

   • Have you forgiven everyone who has hurt you—not because they deserve to be forgiven, but because you deserve peace? If not, ask God to give you grace to forgive them because He has forgiven you.

   • Do you complain about people who have hurt or offended you? Do you tell others what those who have hurt you have done to you? Ask God to help you not spread rumors or speak negatively about them.

   • Think about someone who is hard for you to love and has a need of some sort. How can you meet that need? If you can't think of anything, just wait. Something will probably present itself, and you can determine now that you will help and bless them when a need arises.

   • Do you treat everyone with kindness and respect, even those who are not nice to you—not because *they* are nice, but

because *you* are? If there is someone who is especially difficult to be kind to, how can you show kindness next time you
see them?

- Are you guilty of gloating or secretly rejoicing when certain
people encounter problems or misfortune? Ask God to forgive
you, and commit to being more compassionate in the future.

- Is it taking longer than you would like for you to truly love—
from your heart—someone who is difficult for you to love?
Ask God to help you be patient with the process.

- What kind of good seeds can you sow, meaning how can you
treat people well while you are waiting for your love for someone to grow?

- Many people's comments, actions, and opinions actually
reveal more about how those people view themselves than
about how they view you. Do you tend to take other people's words or actions personally? How can you learn to let
these people not anger you and instead inspire you to grow
stronger?

- When you think of the saying "Hurting people hurt people," do
you think of a specific person? What do you know about that
person that could explain why they treat others, including you,
the way they do? How can you have compassion for them?

- The drama, discouragement, and negativity surrounding you
could serve to limit you, intimidate you, or otherwise hold
you back from becoming the best person you can be. How
can you ignore it or distance yourself from it?

- Controlling people want their behavior to influence your
behavior, but you do not have to allow that to happen. What
one step can you take today to keep someone else's behavior
from determining how you behave?

9. My husband, Dave, treated me with great love for years when I did nothing lovable. What can you learn from his example?

10. Fill in the blanks in these sentences from the last paragraph of chapter 2:

    "Loving people who are hard to love will be _____ on most days and seemingly _____ on some days, but God never asks us to do something without giving us the _____ to do it with _____ help."

11. Do you ever listen to the lie that tells you that loving people is just too hard? What will happen if you believe this?

12. You can love people who are hard to love because God instructs you to do it, He is in you, and He will do it through you. Are you willing to say yes to Him?

Living and Loving by the Word

1. From the beginning of humanity, people have had trouble getting along with each other. Genesis 4 includes the story of the brothers Cain and Abel. Cain was so jealous of Abel that he killed him. How does remembering your flaws help you deal with the flaws of other people?

2. Let me encourage you to memorize Matthew 19:26: "With man this is impossible, but with God all things are possible." Remember this verse and even speak it aloud when you are faced with loving someone you find difficult to love or when you face a challenge of any kind.

3. According to 1 John 4:19, what is the only reason we are able to love God?

What Do You Think?

When you think about a specific person who is hard to love, what is the biggest obstacle to your ability to love them? With God's help, how might you begin to overcome this obstacle?

Take the Love Challenge

When you think of people who are difficult for you to love, someone probably comes to mind immediately. Perhaps you think of several individuals or a certain group of people. I challenge you to love this person or these people in one specific way this week. I'm not suggesting you treat them to an expensive dinner or buy them a nice gift; your act of love may be between you and God, such as praying for them or forgiving them for hurting you. All I'm asking you to do is take one step right now. God will lead you to the next steps in His proper timing and according to His ways.

CHAPTER 3

The Character of Love

Growing in Love

Please read 1 Corinthians 13:4–8 to remind yourself of what this Scripture passage says about love.

1. On a scale of 1 to 10, with 1 being "extremely impatient" and 10 being "extremely patient," how patient do you consider yourself to be?

2. What situations have you been through in your life that have taught you this truth: "Patience is a fruit of the Holy Spirit that only grows under trial"?

3. What random act of kindness can you do today for someone who is hard to love?

4. Take time now to imagine how different the world would be if everyone were kind to one another. What would change?

5. How can you make a positive impact on your personal world by being kind? Now make a plan to act on the ways you believe you can make a difference.

6. The enemy uses jealousy to strain and even destroy relationships. Has this happened to you? Or have you seen it happen to someone else? Describe the situation and write about how it could have been handled better.

7. How does trusting God keep you from being jealous?

8. Fill in the blanks in this sentence from paragraph 4 of the section "Love Is Not Proud or Boastful":

    "Love _____ in giving credit to others and in making them _____ _____."

9. How can you give credit to someone and make them look good this week?

10. Why is pride so damaging to relationships, and why is humility so beneficial to them?

11. Love is not rude; it has good manners. Why is it important to have good manners when building loving relationships?

12. Love is not selfish or self-focused. Have you ever known a selfish person who was truly happy?

13. As we grow in love and learn to become increasingly unselfish, chapter 3 suggests we "begin with one unselfish act each day and build from there." What one unselfish act will you do today?

14. Are you the kind of person who holds grudges or one who lets go of offenses easily? Why is holding grudges so detrimental to individuals and to relationships?

15. How can you practice becoming a person who is impossible to offend?

16. Have you ever chosen not to believe the best about someone and later realized you were wrong? What did you learn from that situation?

17. What impact does being suspicious of someone have on a person's life and relationships? In contrast, what impact does believing the best about someone have on a person's life and relationships?

18. Think about a specific person you find difficult to love. How would believing the best about this person help you enjoy your life more?

19. Fill in the blanks in this sentence from the first paragraph of the section "Love Does Not Rejoice at Injustice and Unrighteousness":

    "People who love always want what is _____ and _____ not only for themselves but also for _____."

20. What situation are you currently involved in that makes you want to stand up for what is right for someone else?

21. What can you do—big or small—to influence people and circumstances around you for good and to advance justice?

22. Really loving people, which includes forgiving them, is not easy, but it is easier than hating them. Can you think of a relationship in which you would be willing to prove this point?

23. Love never fails, and it does not give up on even the most difficult people. Think of the person in your life who is most difficult to love, and take a moment to ask God to help you persevere in loving them and to continue to believe that love never fails.

Living and Loving by the Word

1. How does the opening scripture of chapter 3, which is 1 John 3:18, say we are to love?

2. What does James 1:4 teach you about the benefits of being patient? I suggest reading it in the Amplified Bible.

3. Proverbs 14:30 talks about how destructive jealousy and envy are. According to the second paragraph of the section "Love Is

Not Envious or Jealous," what is the best way to avoid feeling jealous and envious?

4. John 15:13 teaches us that we show our love for others by sacrificing for them. In what circumstance in your life can you sacrifice for someone else, and how can you do it?

5. What do Proverbs 19:11 and Matthew 5:23–24 teach you about not taking offense when people offend you?

6. Think about a situation in which you have been treated wrongly or unjustly. Now pray the words of Psalm 35:22–24: "Lord, you have seen this; do not be silent. Do not be far from me, Lord. Awake, and rise to my defense! Contend for me, my God and Lord. Vindicate me in your righteousness, Lord my God; do not let them gloat over me."

7. Focusing excessively on our faults will distract us, prevent us from growing spiritually, and keep us from doing what God wants us to do. According to Hebrews 12:2, where should we look instead?

What Do You Think?

If you were to write your own description of the character of love based on what you learned in chapter 3, how would you describe it? You may want to write it using words, draw it, take a photograph, or find some other creative representation of what love means to you. You may want to repeat this exercise with other aspects of love.

Take the Love Challenge

Chapter 3 explains the various attributes of love mentioned in 1 Corinthians 13:4–8. I'd like for you to choose your love challenge in this chapter by identifying one of the characteristics of love that is difficult for you to feel and express. Ask God to help you with it and to give you some ideas about how you can grow in it.

PART 2

Love and Peace in Relationships

CHAPTER 4

Becoming a Peacemaker

Growing in Love

1. Make an honest assessment of yourself. Are you a peacemaker in your relationships?

2. When you face conflict in a relationship, how do you respond on a scale of 1 to 10, with 1 being "I run from it as fast as I can" and 10 being "I'm ready for a fight and I won't back down"?

3. Here's your chance to answer a question from the first part of chapter 4: When trouble enters into a relationship, even if you are not the one who started it, do you make an effort to bring peace to the situation?

4. Fill in the blanks in this sentence from the second paragraph of chapter 4:

    "To be a peacemaker, we may have to let someone think we are _____ and say _____ to _____ our point of view."

5. Is being a peacemaker by letting someone think you are wrong and not defending your perspective difficult for you? If so, ask God to give you the wisdom to know when to speak up and when to stay silent, and ask Him to help you remain quiet when you're better off not saying anything.

6. Why are only the spiritually mature able to be peacemakers?

7. As you consider the past week, what are some of the circumstances the enemy has orchestrated or used to steal your peace?

8. Have you been praying for peace when you need to be pursuing it? What is the difference between the two?

9. I believe peace should be one of our top priorities. How important is it to you? How might you make it more of a priority in your life?

10. Can you identify a circumstance in your life when the enemy has set you up to get upset? What did you learn that could help you avoid such situations in the future?

11. When the enemy lies to us, what can we speak to him in order to defeat him?

12. According to paragraph 7 of the section "Pursue Peace," what should be our first line of defense when we encounter trouble in our lives?

13. Fill in the blanks in this sentence from the last line of paragraph 8 in the section "Pursue Peace":

    "When we _____, God _____, but when we _____ without God, He _____."

14. Based on your reading of the section "Peace with God," please answer the following questions:
    • Where does peace begin and why?
    • How do we find peace with God?

15. Loving ourselves in healthy ways is vital to being at peace with ourselves. Do you like yourself? Have you accepted God's love for you? Are you loving yourself in a balanced way? If not, how can you begin to do this?

16. We all sin and make mistakes. When this happens to you, are you quick to repent, receive God's forgiveness, and extend grace to yourself? How could you grow in this area of your life?

17. We do not have to wait for God to finish making the changes we need in ourselves before we feel free to enjoy our lives. Even though you aren't perfect, are you still enjoying your life right now? How could you enjoy it more?

18. Here's your chance to answer a question posed in the section "Peace with Yourself": What is it that you don't like about yourself? With that in mind, what can you do to change it? If you can't change it on your own, remember to pray about it, study what God's Word says about it, and trust Him to do what needs to be done in you.

19. We all do some things right or well, and we do other things wrong or not so well. Make a list of things you do well and a list of things you don't. Which list do you tend to think about most? Let me encourage you to focus on the things you do well. Improve in the things you don't do well, if possible, but do not spend so much time thinking about them that you begin to feel negative about yourself.

20. How can you help yourself feel good about who you are by concentrating on your strengths and not your weaknesses?

21. What are "power thoughts"? List three specific power thoughts that will add peace to your life instead taking it away.

22. What are your peace stealers? Remember, when you are aware of them, you can pray about them and ask God to help you guard against them.

Living and Loving by the Word

1. According to Matthew 5:9, what is the benefit of being a peacemaker?

2. In Philippians 2:2–8, Paul mentions several keys to unity with Christ and peaceful relationships with others. What are they?

3. What advice does Paul offer in 2 Timothy 2:23–24, and why?

4. How do Isaiah 9:6 and Ephesians 2:14 refer to Jesus?

5. In Mark 4:39, Jesus calmed a raging storm simply by speaking to it. Why was He able to do this?

6. In the Amplified Bible, Classic Edition, Colossians 3:15 reads:

   And let the peace (soul harmony which comes) from Christ rule (act as umpire continually) in your hearts [deciding and settling with finality all questions that arise in your minds, in that peaceful state] to which as [members of Christ's] one body you were also called [to live]. And be thankful (appreciative), [giving praise to God always].

   What does it mean to let peace "act as umpire" in your life?

7. Based on Ephesians 6:10–18, what are the keys to effective spiritual warfare?

8. How does Philippians 1:6 encourage you?

9. This is the scripture I meditate on and speak aloud when I feel myself beginning to worry. Maybe you'd like to memorize it so you can think about it and speak it when you feel anxious.

   Do not be anxious about anything, but in every situation, by prayer and petition, with thanksgiving, present your requests to God. And the peace of God, which transcends all understanding, will guard your hearts and your minds in Christ Jesus.

Philippians 4:6–7

10. According to Romans 14:17, what does God's Kingdom consist of?

What Do You Think?

When people think of peace, they think of different things. Some visualize the beach. Some think of sitting by a fire in a fireplace wrapped in a blanket in a quiet house on a cold day. Some think of the absence of conflict in family relationships. Some think of freedom from war. What do you think of when you think of peace?

Take the Love Challenge

Consider a specific situation or relationship in your life that was once peaceful and is now tense (not dangerous, just not peaceful). I challenge you to act on the spiritual maturity God has given you and take one step toward restoring peace, even if you don't feel like doing it.

CHAPTER 5

The Danger of Anger

Growing in Love

1. As you think back over the past several years, have you noticed an increase in anger among people around you? Have you noticed an increase in anger in yourself?

2. Can you see how anger may be rooted in fear? Do you personally feel angry about something and realize that the anger comes from fear? How can you reduce your anger by dealing with your fear?

3. What does anger solve?

4. Do you believe that the real reason many people are angry is that they are trying to live apart from God? Think of someone you know who is angry and far from God. Take a moment to pray for that person right now.

5. Why is the following statement true: "God's love takes away our anger when we are in right relationship with Him"?

6. Have you ever known anyone who was jealous of another person's position of leadership and influence, like Eliab? Did that situation turn out well for the person who was jealous?

7. Have you ever known anyone who was jealous because they were afraid someone would try to take something that belonged to them, like King Saul? How did that situation end up?

8. Have you witnessed or experienced firsthand the destructive power of fear, jealousy, or anger? What did you learn from it?

9. According to the second paragraph of the section "Is Anger a Sin?," what is the best course of action to take when you are angry with someone?

10. When you become angry, why is it important to deal with the anger right away?

11. Are you angry with yourself sometimes? What is the best way to handle this, according to the first paragraph of the section "Are You Angry with Yourself?" I encourage you to take time to think through the situations, failures, mistakes, or sins that may be causing you to be angry with yourself and to deal with each one so you can move forward in life.

12. Have you ever noticed yourself becoming angry with someone else when actually you are angry with yourself? How can you make things right with that person?

13. Some people feel that life is not fair to them. Sometimes this is true, and sometimes it is just their perception. Do you feel this way? If so, let me encourage you to turn the pain and injustice over to God and let Him be your vindicator.

14. If you are angry and you know the source of your anger, write it down. If you are angry and don't know the source, the "Take the Love Challenge" section at the end of this chapter can help you identify it. Ask God to show you the source of your anger, and trust Him to reveal it to you when the time is right.

15. What is the difference between expressed anger and repressed anger? Can you identify one or both of these types of anger in your life?

16. What are some of the problems that result from repressed anger? What problems or struggles have you personally encountered that may be rooted in repressed anger?

17. Wounded healers cannot be very effective. Why is it important for people to allow God to heal them first before they begin trying to help others find healing?

18. What is the only good kind of anger, and how would you describe it? Have you ever felt it? If so, what happened, and how did you feel about it?

19. What causes you to feel righteous anger?

Living and Loving by the Word

1. I encourage you to memorize, meditate on, and speak aloud this verse: "Perfect love casts out fear" (1 John 4:18 NKJV).

2. What does Ephesians 4:26–27 teach you about being angry?

3. Fill in the blanks:

    James 1:19–20 teaches us to be "quick to _____, slow to _____ and _____ to become _____."

4. According to Ecclesiastes 7:9, where does anger lodge?

5. Proverbs 16:32 (AMPC) says: "He who is slow to anger is better than the mighty, he who rules his [own] spirit than he who takes a city." What does this verse mean? Why is it important to remember this?

6. The Bible teaches us not to make friends with angry and hot-tempered people and advises us not even to associate with

people who are easily angered (Proverbs 22:24–25). Think about your friends and acquaintances right now. Are they peaceful people, or are they angry people?

7. First Peter 3:11 (AMPC) helps us understand the order in which peace must come in our lives. What is it?

8. Jesus demonstrated righteous anger on at least two occasions, according to Matthew 21:12–13 and Mark 3:1–6. What were the circumstances of each instance?

What Do You Think?

I believe the opening quotation of chapter 5 helps us understand what is happening in the world today. As you follow the news, and even as you look at your own family or community, what do you think about Edward Albert's observation: "Fear is the only true enemy, born of ignorance and the parent of anger and hate"?

Take the Love Challenge

In order to move beyond anger, it's necessary to clearly identify the source of it. I challenge you to do that. Check below any of the common sources of anger people deal with, and if you don't see the cause of your anger, write it below the list. Who are you angry with?

- God
- Yourself
- A spouse or former spouse
- A family member or former family member
- A friend
- An abuser

- A situation in which you were mistreated
- A person who mistreated you
- A boss or work colleague
- Someone who stole from you
- Someone who spread lies about you
- Someone who abandoned you
- A mistake or bad decision you made—or one that someone else made that affected you negatively
- A church, organization, or workplace
- The world's system
- People whose beliefs or opinions are different from yours
- People who have more than you have or have gotten something you wanted
- A significant loss
- Life in general
- Other _____

Name your anger, release it, turn it over to God, forgive the offender (if you are angry with a person), ask God for justice, and move on with your life. The longer you put off doing this, the longer you hold yourself captive to anger and misery, because angry people are miserable people. It's time to be free.

CHAPTER 6

Disagree Agreeably

Growing in Love

1. On a scale of 1 to 10, with 1 being "practically no one" and 10 being "almost everyone," how many of the people in your life do you typically agree with?

2. How do you tend to respond in a conversation when you realize you disagree with someone? Check all that apply (you may feel more comfortable disagreeing with some people than with others).

   - I find a way to get away from them.
   - I quickly change the subject, but remain in conversation.
   - I know my opinion but creatively avoid expressing it.
   - I find a way to express some disagreement but hide the extent of it.
   - I let them know I respect their right to their opinion, then calmly and clearly state my opinion.

   Which of these do you think is the healthiest way to respond, and how can you grow in it?

3. What does it mean to disagree agreeably?

4. What type of person do you respect more? Check one.

   - One who tries to manipulate me into agreeing with them.

- One who shames me for not agreeing with them.
- One who clearly expresses and explains their disagreement with my opinion but doesn't try to manipulate or shame me.

Are you this kind of person?

5. Dave and I found a way to disagree agreeably when he agreed to let me decorate our home, and I agreed that he would have the larger office with the better view. Have you ever compromised in a similar way? If so, how did it work out? If not, I encourage you to consider doing it in the future.

6. Do you struggle to understand how some people can have the opinions they hold? Have you accepted the fact that we all have different perspectives and that every person is free to have their unique point of view? How can you work toward not allowing opinions that do not align with yours frustrate you so you can keep your relationships peaceful?

7. When people are talking about a topic on which everyone does not agree, what is the difference between a discussion and an argument? How can you help keep discussions from becoming arguments?

8. Fill in the blank from this sentence in paragraph 5 of chapter 6:
   "Learning to disagree agreeably is rooted in _____."
   What does this mean to you?

9. Has someone ever tried to push you into saying that what they are doing is right, even though you acknowledge their right to do it but you know it violates God's Word? How did you handle that situation? Could you agree to disagree and still be cordial toward each other? That's the goal.

10. For you, is there any issue or topic of conversation worth ruining a relationship over? I hope not. You can always say, "We obviously disagree about this matter, so let's agree not to

discuss it and to talk about things that will help us keep the peace in our relationship."

11. Fill in the blanks, referring to the first sentence of the section "Even When You Think You Are Right, You Could Be Wrong": "I think I'm _____, but I _____ be _____." Is there a situation in your life right now in which this statement could help keep the peace or even save a relationship?

12. Why is the statement "I think I'm right, but I could be wrong" described as "nine powerful words that disarm the evil spirit that is trying to bring division among people"? How can these words help prevent an argument?

13. How have you found the following quote from John Ruskin to be true? "It is better to lose your pride with someone you love rather than to lose that someone you love with your useless pride."

14. Have you ever been right in a situation but regretted it because of what it cost you in a relationship with someone you love? What did you learn through that experience?

15. Based on what you learned in chapter 6, what advice would you give yourself next time you feel tempted to insist that you are right about something?

16. How could this advice lead to greater peace in a circumstance in your life: "When two people disagree about a decision that must be made, the one who is in authority should be the one to make it"?

17. Why do people who are insecure try so hard to prove they are right?

18. What are some of the problems that insecurity causes? How have you experienced this personally or seen it in others? How did it affect you?

19. What are the benefits of feeling secure in Christ? How do we find that security in Him?

20. If you have adult children, is it hard for you to stop managing their lives? If you are having difficulty with this issue, ask God to help you trust Him for their well-being.

21. Why is it so important to give your adult children freedom and let them make their own mistakes, even when you could help them avoid those mistakes?

Living and Loving by the Word

1. According to Proverbs 16:18, pride leads to destruction. How have you seen or experienced pride destroying a relationship?

2. Since pride leads to destruction, according to Proverbs 16:18, we can deduce that humility in relationships brings strength and healing. How have you observed or experienced this?

3. First Peter 5:6 teaches us that we are to humble ourselves under God's mighty hand, and He will lift us up at the proper time. If we need to be shown to be right in a situation, God can easily arrange that. How have you seen God show you to be right in a situation in your life? What did you learn from this experience that encouraged you to simply be humble and let Him work?

4. According to Philippians 2:5–8, what kind of mind should be in us? Why?

5. Insecure people often brag about their accomplishments, their possessions, the people they know, their job, or their education. Yet none of these can bring them the security they long for. Philippians 3:3 says we have only one reason to boast. What is it?

What Do You Think?

In the section "Peace Is More Valuable than Being Right," I write about a disagreement between Dave and me, one that made me feel bad physically for two days. The topic of our argument wasn't worth the price I paid emotionally and physically to defend my perspective. What do you think about that? Do you believe peace truly is more valuable than being right?

Take the Love Challenge

Can you think of someone who seems to enjoy disagreeing with you? Perhaps you feel that no matter how you try to avoid topics you know are divisive, they seem to steer the conversation toward something they know the two of you do not agree on. You soon feel ambushed and perhaps even verbally abused because of their attack on your opinion. Next time this happens, I challenge you to say something like "Right now that's not what we're talking about, so let's stay focused on this topic until we finish the conversation. We know we disagree on this other topic, and I value my relationship with you enough to decide not to discuss it."

Avoiding Strife

Growing in Love

1. In the first sentence of chapter 7, what words and phrases are used to describe strife?

2. After you read chapter 7, did you realize you have been living in strife-filled situations without knowing what to call them? What are they?

3. Have you ever been part of a group of people or an organization that was destroyed by strife? What happened?

4. What is the only way to stop strife?

5. When we find ourselves dealing with strife, we can either feed it or stop it. How do we feed it? And how do we stop it?

6. When someone tells you something negative about another person, how do you typically respond? Check one.
   - Believe it immediately and then tell someone.
   - Think, *Well, I can see how that might be true*, and then ask other people if they have heard the same thing.
   - Ask the person where they heard it and refuse to believe it without going directly to the person to whom it pertains. If it is not true, you tell the person spreading the rumor and ask them to stop.

What is the best way to respond? If you are not currently doing this, will you commit to start doing it right away? What will be your first step?

7. How do we know that strife and division are works of the enemy?

8. Before you read chapter 7, had you thought about the fact that, generally speaking, the news media and much of social media stay busy spreading mostly bad news? Would you consider limiting your exposure to bad news? How could you increase the amount of good news you watch, read, or listen to each day?

9. Based on what you read in the first paragraph of the section "Anything We Don't Feed Doesn't Live Very Long," what is the highest calling on your life?

10. How can keeping strife out of our individual lives help heal our troubled world?

11. Everyone can be hard to love at some time or another, including you and me. What about yourself do you think makes you hard for people to love sometimes? How can you improve in this area?

12. Think about someone close to you and the things that make them difficult to love at times. How can you change your perspective on this issue, be more merciful and forgiving toward it, or focus less on it and more on this person's good qualities? How will this help you enjoy your relationship with them?

13. According to the section "That They Might Be One," what does "being one" mean? What does it *not* mean?

14. Fill in the blanks in these sentences from the last paragraph of the section "That They Might Be One":

"Oneness is based on a _____ we make to find places of _____ and _____ on them in our relationships. Of course, this requires _____ and _____."

15. Here's your chance to answer two questions you find at the end of the section "That They Might Be One":

   • Are you willing to make oneness and unity a main goal in your life?

   • Will you make the effort to live in unity for Christ's sake and for the glory of His Kingdom?

16. Why does focusing on people's good points instead of their negative traits help us stay out of strife? Make a list of the good qualities about someone you don't always find easy to get along with.

17. What did you learn in chapter 7 about the dangers of strife and the importance of dealing with it swiftly and decisively?

Living and Loving by the Word

1. Resentment, hatred, and bitterness lead to strife. According to Hebrews 12:15 (AMPC), if they are allowed to fester, what happens to people? If you have seen this happen, describe the situation.

2. Unity is the opposite and the absence of strife. According to Psalm 133, what can those who walk in unity expect?

3. What can you learn about strife from 2 Timothy 2:23–24 (AMPC)?

4. What do Matthew 7:12 and John 13:34 teach us about how to relate to people?

5. In Genesis 13, what happened as a result of Abram's refusal to allow strife between his herdsmen and those of his nephew Lot?
6. What does Paul teach us in 1 Corinthians 1:10 and Ephesians 4:1–3 about getting along with other people?
7. What does Genesis 2:24 teach about husbands and wives?

What Do You Think?

In chapter 7 of *Loving People Who Are Hard to Love*, I shared three of our values at Joyce Meyer Ministries:

• Always walk in integrity, which means to always do what we say we will do, always be honest with the money over which God makes us stewards, and always tell the truth.
• Do whatever we do with excellence, to the best of our ability, and always go the extra mile.
• Keep strife out of our marriage, family, and ministry.

If you are a leader in a church, ministry, business, or civic organization, what would you think about adopting these values for your group? You could even do it for your family. You may have to change some of the words, but you can easily apply these principles in a variety of settings. If you work for yourself, you can adapt them for your business. If you are not a leader and you are not in a position of great influence right now, you can still choose to live by these values personally. Why not?

Take the Love Challenge

I challenge you to become known as a strife stopper instead of a strife spreader and commit to not repeat the negative information you hear about other people unless, for some important reason, someone truly needs to know it. Be the person with whom strife spreaders do not want to share rumors or bad reports, because they know you will confront the strife they want to create and challenge them to stop spreading it. I also challenge you to become a person who spreads as much positive, uplifting news and information as you possibly can to everyone in your sphere of influence.

CHAPTER 8

Love Is Not Easily Offended

Growing in Love

1. Fill in the blanks in the third sentence of chapter 8:
   "Anytime we are overly _____ on how we feel, we are likely to find a reason to feel _____, _____, _____, _____, _____, and a host of other_____ emotions."

2. What do we need to believe about people that will help us not to be so easily offended by them?

3. Have you ever been offended and the person who offended you did not even know you were upset? Who did your negative emotions hurt—you or the other person?

4. Fill in the blanks from paragraph 3 of chapter 8:
   "Satan wants us _____. He wants division, but God wants _____, _____, and _____."

5. The English word *offense* comes from what Greek word? What does this Greek word mean?

6. Why is offense often called Satan's bait?

7. Here's your chance to answer the question in the section "Satan's Bait": Are you angry or offended with God because something you wanted has not happened, or because you have had to endure difficulty that you cannot understand?

8. If you are offended with God because of some trial He has allowed to happen in your life or because He has not yet done something you want Him to do for you, do you think you really have any right to be offended? Has it occurred to you that He loves you more than anyone and wants only the very best for you?

9. If you are offended with God, I urge you to ask His forgiveness and to recommit yourself to trusting Him fully. Know that His only motivation regarding what happens in your life is love and that when you face difficulty, He is the only one who can help you gain victory over it and the only one who can heal you from the pain it may inflict.

10. Fill in the blanks in this sentence from paragraph 6 of the section "Satan's Bait":

    "When we _____, we are dangerous to the devil; when we don't, he is _____ to us."

11. According to the first paragraph of the section "Choose Wisdom above Emotion," what do wise people do?

12. How does seeing people from God's perspective enable us to love them?

13. As you think about your life right now, are there any ways in which your love has grown cold? Are there any specific people toward whom you feel your love is less fervent than it needs to be? How can you grow in having and demonstrating fervent love to others?

14. We are to put on love and to take off attitudes that do not reflect love. What attitudes are you wearing right now, so to speak, that you need to take off so you can put on love?

15. As a reminder, love is not a feeling; it is the way we treat people. Is there someone in your life who has offended you recently? How could you deliberately show love to that person this week?

Living and Loving by the Word

1. According to Psalm 37:37, what awaits those who seek peace?
2. What does 1 Peter 5:8 teach us about our enemy, the devil?
3. According to Mark 4:17 in the Amplified Bible, Classic Edition, what can happen to young Christians or weak believers when trouble comes their way?
4. In Philippians 1:9–10 (NKJV), what does Paul pray for the church?
5. According to Proverbs 4:23, why is it so important to guard our hearts?
6. Based on Psalm 119:165, what can we expect if we love God's Word (or His law)?
7. Romans 14:12 says we will all give an account of our lives to God someday. The primary thing He wants us to do is to love other people. Will you be able to say that, with His help, you loved them to the best of your ability?
8. What do we learn about loving other people from John 13:34–35 and Romans 13:10?
9. What does the parable of the wheat and the weeds, found in Matthew 13:24–30, teach us?

10. According to 1 Peter 4:8, what does love do?

11. In Proverbs 25:21–22, what do the burning coals represent? How can you heap burning coals on someone's head in a situation in your life right now?

12. When the enemy tries to tell you someone is simply too hard to love, how do you know that is a lie, based on John 8:44 and Matthew 19:26?

What Do You Think?

After reading chapter 8, why do you think understanding offense and resisting it are so important? What do you think our world would look like if people simply refused to be offended? Let's make this personal: What do you think *your* world would look like if *you* simply refuse to be offended from this moment forward?

Take the Love Challenge

Chapter 8 includes the story of a woman who spent one week counting how many times she found herself in situations in which she could have been offended. She counted forty times. Because she was familiar with this teaching on avoiding strife, she did not take the bait of the offense one time. I challenge you to follow her example. Take one week and count how many opportunities you have to be offended. Pay attention to how many times the enemy tries to steal your peace, bring division into a relationship, and keep you from loving people. Every time Satan gives you a chance to be offended, resist!

CHAPTER 9

What Is Your Opinion?

Growing in Love

1. According to the first sentence of chapter 9, what is the definition of an opinion?

2. Some people are more opinionated than others, meaning that they think or feel more strongly about issues or situations than others do. On a scale of 1 to 10, with 1 being "not opinionated at all" and 10 being "extremely opinionated," how opinionated do you consider yourself?

3. Some people can keep their opinions to themselves, while others are eager to tell everyone around them what they think. On a scale of 1 to 10, with 1 being "not important at all" and 10 being "extremely important," how important is it for you to share your opinion with others?

4. Do you tend to share your opinions primarily with people you expect to agree with you? Or do you talk about what you think with anyone who will listen?

5. Here's your chance to answer a question asked in the first section of chapter 9: Given the fact that an opinion is nothing more than what someone thinks, what is an opinion really worth? How important should people's opinions be to you?

6. Fill in the blanks from this sentence in the second paragraph of chapter 9:

   "A person's opinion _____ be _____, but it may be _____."

7. When you seek opinions from other people, do you ask for input from various individuals and consider everything they have said, or do you allow one person's opinion to influence you more than it should?

8. Have you ever let other people's opinions run your life or made a decision based solely on what other people thought you should do? Is this the way you want to live in the future?

9. Have you ever allowed someone else's opinion to become your reality or affect your sense of value or self-worth? Why is this not a good way to live, and what can you do to change it?

10. People tend to start many sentences with "I think…" Why do so many people want to tell others what they think?

11. Consider taking an informal survey over the next day or so. Pay attention to how many times you hear someone say "I think." Then, pay attention to how many times *you* say "I think." You can't do anything about what other people say, but when you hear "I think," you can remind yourself that they are only speaking an opinion, which may or may not be right.

12. Fill in the blanks in this sentence from the second paragraph of the section "I Think":

   "We live in a _____ world, and much of the strife arises because people offer their _____ and are then offended if others do not _____ or _____ it."

13. Have you ever witnessed or been involved in a situation in which two people or groups have differing opinions and are unable to respect their differences, leading to broken relationships? Describe the situation and suggest some ways the people involved could be respectful of each other and save their relationship.

14. How do you respond when you offer your opinion and people do not accept it or agree with it? Do you press your point, or do you say something like "Let's accept that we see this issue differently, but let's not argue about it"?

15. Are you guilty of forming and/or vocalizing opinions about other people in the following areas? Check all that apply:
    - What they say
    - What they do
    - What they post on social media
    - What they wear
    - What issues they support or don't support
    - Where they live
    - Where they went to school (or currently go to school)
    - Where they go to church
    - How they spend their money
    - How they spend their time
    - What they choose to eat
    - How much they exercise or don't exercise
    - Which movies or television shows they choose to watch
    - Which sports teams they cheer for
    - What kind of technology they use or how recent it is

Are you surprised by how many you checked? Will you commit to loving people as they are and accepting the choices they make, without forming and sharing your opinions about them?

16. According to the section "I Think," what do we have to do if we want to enjoy peace?

17. In what ways do you think social media has become a dangerous form of communication? Why?

18. On a scale of 1 to 10, with 1 being "practically never" and 10 being "almost always," how often do you research, fact check, or otherwise investigate what you read on social media?

19. How can you improve in verifying or checking into what you read on social media before you choose to believe it?

20. According to the section "Social Media," what is one of the dangers of mean-spirited gossip?

21. What if every word you spoke about someone else was the kind of word you would like spoken of you? How much would your conversation about people change?

22. What can you learn from the section "David, a Man after God's Own Heart"?

Living and Loving by the Word

1. How does the apostle Paul encourage us to live in 1 Thessalonians 4:11 (AMPC)?

2. How is 1 John 4:1 (MSG) relevant to your life today, especially where social media is concerned?

3. What do gossips and busybodies do, according to 1 Timothy 5:13 (ESV)?

4. Have you ever thought about how powerful your words are? What does Proverbs 11:9 (ESV) say our mouths are powerful enough to do?

5. According to Proverbs 26:20–22 (ESV), how can we stop the spread of rumors and gossip?

6. Romans 1:29–32 (ESV) is a sobering passage of Scripture. In light of it, what changes might you need to make to your thoughts and behavior, especially the way you use your words?

7. Forming opinions leads to passing judgment. What does the story in John 8:1–11 teach us about judging others?

8. Fill in the blank, based on 1 Samuel 16:7:

   People judge us according to the flesh, but God looks at the

   _____.

9. Based on Matthew 7:1–2, what kind of harvest will we reap if we judge others?

What Do You Think?

In chapter 9, I mention that some people are wise enough to keep their opinions to themselves unless someone asks for them. This indicates that sharing an opinion without being asked may be unwise. Why do you think that sharing your opinion only when someone wants to hear it is wise? Why do you think offering your opinion when people haven't asked for it is unwise?

Take the Love Challenge

I believe one reason the world seems to be such an angry, volatile place these days is that people seem to be almost shouting over one another to express their opinions in many situations. This chapter's love challenge is simple: I challenge you to withhold what you think about people or circumstances unless someone asks for your opinion. Instead of offering an opinion, which could be divisive, find a way to say something that brings peace and unity into a situation instead. Next time you are tempted to offer an unsolicited opinion on something, remember this chapter and this challenge.

Are You Angry with Yourself?

Growing in Love

1. What is a major reason so many people in the world are angry?

2. Do you know people who are angry with themselves and, because of this, their anger is expressed toward others? Will you pray for these people and ask God to help them forgive themselves?

3. Based on the first section of chapter 10, how does a life of sin and disobedience to God contribute to anger?

4. What kinds of things result in a guilty conscience?

5. Why is having a guilty conscience such a problem?

6. Why do people who have a guilty conscience deflect their feelings by finding fault with other people?

7. Have you ever engaged in blame shifting? Is blame shifting helpful to people? Why or why not?

8. Why is taking responsibility for our attitudes, words, and actions important?

9. Are you currently in a relationship with someone who is often angry and expresses anger outwardly in various ways, but is actually angry with themself? How can this understanding help you pray for this person?

10. What is the difference between knowing Jesus as our Savior and knowing Him as our Lord? Do you relate to Him as Savior and Lord?

11. What are some of the benefits of relating to Jesus as Lord?

12. According to paragraph 4 of the section "Is Jesus Your Savior and Your Lord?," what is the best way to live free from guilt?

13. Fill in the blanks in this sentence from paragraph 4 of the section "Is Jesus Your Savior and Your Lord?":

    "Repentance is not merely saying 'I'm sorry I sinned,' but _____ your _____ and _____ your _____. It means turning from _____ _____ _____ way and going _____ way."

14. The Holy Spirit, who lives inside all believers, is often depicted as a dove. What does this represent?

15. When you consider the fact that the Holy Spirit can be grieved by what we say, is there anything or anyone you know you need to stop speaking negatively about?

16. Is there a topic of conversation or a way of speaking (gossip, complaining, criticizing, coarse language, or other unwholesome talk) you realize you should not engage in anymore?

17. Paragraph 4 of the section "Do Not Offend the Holy Spirit" lists several things that grieve Him. What are they? Are any of these a regular part of your life? If so, how can you eliminate them?

18. Why does a guilty conscience hinder effective prayer?

19. Is there any hidden sin in your heart? Remember, God knows all about it. If you will simply admit it to Him and ask His forgiveness, He will immediately forgive you and cleanse you of the guilt and condemnation of it.

20. What can you learn from King David's life about trying to ignore or hide sin?

21. Fill in the blanks in this sentence from the first paragraph of the section "Maintaining a Clean Conscience":

Our conscience "condemns what is _____ and _____ what is _____."

22. According to the second paragraph of "Maintaining a Clean Conscience," what is false guilt, and how can we break free from it or avoid feeling it in the first place?

23. Based on the last sentence of the section "Maintaining a Clean Conscience," what is the only way to keep a clean conscience?

24. What does the story of Daniel teach you about following your conscience?

25. What can you learn from Joseph about refusing to compromise?

26. When we feel we need to hide something we are doing, what does that tell us?

27. Why is it important to call sin what it is, confront it boldly, and deal with it harshly?

Living and Loving by the Word

1. What can you learn about a guilty conscience from this chapter's opening scripture, 1 John 3:21 (AMPC)?

2. Why is knowing James 4:17 and applying it to your life important?

3. How do the following verses help us understand that even when we feel guilty about something, we do not need to punish ourselves?
   • Hebrews 9:14
   • Hebrews 10:17–18
   • 1 Peter 2:24

4. Fill in the blanks in Galatians 2:20:

 "I have been _____ with Christ and I no longer live, but _____ lives in me. The life I now live in the body, I live by _____ in the Son of God, who _____ me and gave _____ for _____."

5. John 14:26 (AMPC) teaches us that the Holy Spirit is our Comforter. In the first paragraph of the section "Do Not Offend the Holy Spirit," what six words appear in parentheses, as the amplification of "Comforter," to help us understand the ministry of the Holy Spirit in our lives?

6. What additional roles does the Holy Spirit play in our lives, according to John 16:8?

7. Ephesians 4:30 tells us not to grieve the Holy Spirit. Based on the Amplified Bible, Classic Edition translation of this verse, what does it mean to grieve Him?

8. According to Ephesians 4:29 (AMPC), what are some ways we can grieve the Holy Spirit?

9. How does Ephesians 4:32 say we should treat people?

10. Please read Hebrews 4:15–16 in the section "Conscience and Confidence." What will we receive when we approach God's throne of grace with confidence?

11. According to Hebrews 12:1, how are we to deal with sin?

What Do You Think?

In chapter 10, you read: "When God forgives our sin, He also removes the guilt of it, but letting go of the guilt is often difficult for us." What do you think? Have you found letting go of guilt difficult? If so, why? To help you release the guilt you feel, let

me encourage you to meditate on the following scriptures and to
pray and ask God to help you completely break free from guilt.

- 1 John 1:9
- John 3:16
- Isaiah 54:4
- Micah 7:19
- 1 John 2:1

Take the Love Challenge

As you read this challenge, you may think it sounds easy, but it
may take time and effort—and it *will* take the help of the Holy
Spirit. It's this: Forgive yourself and love yourself.

Let It Go

Growing in Love

1. According to the first sentence of chapter 11, there is no hope of loving anyone at all unless we are willing to do what?

2. Fill in the blanks in the second sentence of chapter 11:

   "No one on this earth can have a relationship and never _____, _____, or _____ another."

3. When you think about forgiving people who have hurt you, does a certain person immediately come to mind? This person is a prime candidate for your forgiveness, and I encourage you to keep them in mind throughout this chapter, trusting God to help you forgive them.

4. Have you ever thought someone was perfect or nearly perfect, only to find out they weren't? Describe that situation.

5. Why is it true that you do yourself a favor when you forgive those who have hurt or wronged you?

6. Fill in the blanks in this sentence from the second paragraph of chapter 11:

   "Yet, I believe _____ gains more ground in most Christians' lives through _____ than through any other means."

7. Why is it impossible to truly love people without being generous with forgiveness?

8. I mention that I was "a great accountant of offenses." Do you hold on to offenses or hold grudges against people? Or are you able to quickly let go of the hurts or offenses people have caused you? Which is the better way to live?

9. Why does real love forget how it has been hurt?

10. Do you know anyone whose relationship with God is being negatively affected by unforgiveness toward another human being? How can you pray for that person to be able to forgive?

11. We can't limit unforgiveness in our hearts to the person who hurt or wronged us. If unforgiveness is in our hearts, it affects us in many ways. Have you ever known someone who refuses to forgive in a specific relationship and then wonders why they struggle in other relationships too? Describe the situation.

12. As followers of Christ, why must we forgive?

13. What does the third sentence of the second paragraph of the section "It Isn't an Option" say unforgiveness is like? Why is this true? Have you had personal experience with this?

14. How does unforgiveness hinder our relationship with God?

15. Why is it important to search our hearts and make sure we are free from unforgiveness before we pray?

16. Why does forgiveness sometimes feel unfair to the person who has been hurt?

17. Have you seen evidence of the saying "Hurting people hurt people"? How have you experienced this?

18. Fill in the blanks in these sentences from the second paragraph of the section "It's Not Fair":

"When people hurt God's children, He will be our _____ and will _____ the offenses

against us if we _____ them go and leave
them to _____ to deal with. He is a God
of _____, and in due time, He will make
_____ everything that is _____."

19. How is forgiveness "the beginning of healing for the wounded
soul and the brokenhearted person"?

20. Why is letting go of the past necessary to moving forward in
life?

21. The first step in the process of forgiveness is choosing to obey
God's instruction to forgive. We start by praying and asking
Him to help us forgive. Under the heading "Choose to Obey
God," what does the second paragraph say about how to pray
and what to pray for?

22. The second step in the process of forgiveness is not speaking
negatively about those who have wounded or wronged you.
Why is this important?

23. The third step in the process of forgiveness is helping those
who have hurt or offended you if they need help. What is
something practical you can do to help someone who has hurt
you or for someone who is hard for you to love?

24. Do you tend to base decisions about whether to forgive people
on how you feel toward them? Describe a time when your
feelings easily deceived you.

25. How often and how many times should you forgive people?

Living and Loving by the Word

1. As human beings, when we have forgiven an offense, we often
still struggle to keep from mentioning it again. But God deals

differently with our past sins. What does Zephaniah 3:17 (AMPC) say about this?

2. What does 1 Corinthians 13:5 (AMPC) mean when it says that love "takes no account of the evil done to it"?

3. What does Matthew 6:15 teach about the connection between our forgiving others and God's forgiving us?

4. Please read Colossians 3:13 (ESV). What does this verse say about forgiving other people?

5. According to Mark 11:25, what is the relationship between forgiveness and answered prayer?

6. What does Romans 2:4 say about God's kindness? Why should this keep us from being jealous if He blesses people who have hurt us in the past?

7. What does Romans 12:20 teach us to do as we walk through the process of forgiving our enemies?

What Do You Think?

In chapter 11, you read several real-life stories of people who chose to forgive in situations where forgiveness did not seem fair to them. These are "The Unlikely Pardoner," "The Understanding Widower," and "The Compassionate Officer." Choose one of these stories and put yourself into it. What do you think you would have done under the circumstances?

Take the Love Challenge

I challenge you to ask God to lead you on a journey of forgiveness and freedom. Take time to think through your life—as far back as you can remember—and ask God to help you recall any unforgiveness that lingers in your heart as a result of situations that were painful to you. Think about the people involved and ask yourself if you have honestly forgiven each one completely. If you still feel pain, anger, or resentment when you think of them, it indicates a need to forgive. Remember, forgiveness is a choice, not an emotion, so you can forgive someone by making a decision, whether your feelings support it or not. You may want to refer to the section "Understanding the Process of Forgiveness" to lead you through these acts of forgiveness that will set you free.

PART 3

The Power of Love and Acceptance

CHAPTER 12

Can't You Be More Like Me?

Growing in Love

1. According to the first sentence of chapter 12, what is an important key to being able to love people?

2. On a scale of 1 to 10, with 1 being "not much at all" and 10 being "very much," how much do you really accept people as they are? If your score is low, how can you grow in your willingness to accept others unconditionally?

3. Is accepting people as they are the same as condoning bad behavior or accepting the sin in their lives? What's the difference?

4. According to the first paragraph of chapter 12, what does it mean to accept people the way they are?

5. Why is trying to force someone to change useless?

6. Have you ever depended on someone else to make you feel a certain way, as I depended on Dave during the early years of our marriage?

7. What can you learn about unconditional love and acceptance from the way Dave treated me when I was difficult to love?

8. Have you ever tried to manipulate someone into changing so they would be more like you wanted them to be? People do

this using guilt, anger, pouting, the silent treatment, and other unhealthy ways. If you've done it, how did you choose to do it? Did it lead to a stronger relationship?

9. Has anyone ever tried to manipulate you into becoming who they wanted you to be instead of allowing you to be who you are? How did you respond? What did you learn about this type of situation in chapter 12?

10. Have you ever believed, as I once did, that your bad behavior was the result of what someone else did or didn't do? Why is this not true?

11. Have you ever thought, *If only (name) would change, I would be happy*? Why is this not true?

12. Does true change come from the outside in, or from the inside out?

13. Is there anyone in your life you really wish you could change? Are you trying to change them yourself, or are you praying for them and trusting God to do what needs to be done in them?

14. How does trying to change someone send a message of rejection, not acceptance?

15. Why is working with the Holy Spirit, allowing Him to change you into the person God wants you to be, and expressing love and acceptance to other people better than trying to change them?

16. Think about the people closest to you—perhaps your family members or your best friends. What are some unique characteristics of each one? How are their differences a blessing in your life? How can you show each one how much you love and value them?

17. Think about this statement from paragraph four of the section "Who Are You Trying to Change?": "If we were successful in

conforming others to our image, we wouldn't be able to find anyone we liked." Do you believe this is accurate? Why?

18. If you have children or other significant young people in your life, how are you praying for them? Are you asking God to help them become who *you* want them to become or who *He* wants them to become? Write a heartfelt prayer for each of the young people in your life, asking God to shape them into the people He wants them to be.

19. Is there someone you are trying to change who may actually have the very strengths you need to compensate for your weaknesses, and vice versa? How could the two of you work together to accomplish something you could never do on your own?

20. Here's your chance to think about the question at the end of the section "Who Are You Trying to Change?": Trying to change other people is hard labor and very frustrating because it never works, so why not enjoy the aspects that you can enjoy in people and leave the rest to God?

21. In practical ways, how can you enjoy the relationship you have with someone and simply trust God without trying to change that person?

22. Why is trying to change ourselves when we realize how far we fall short of God's ideal not a good thing to do?

23. When you need to change, God will do the changing. How can you enjoy yourself and your life while He is working on you?

24. Are you ever too uptight about your faults and lose your joy over things that God will change in you eventually? How can you relax and not worry about the things you are trusting God to change?

25. What does it mean to turn yourself over to God?

26. How can you love the people around you in their imperfect state, just as God loves you in your imperfect state?

27. Think about a few people you really want to change. How can you set them free to be themselves while you trust God to change them as He sees fit?

28. In paragraph 5 of the section "The Gift of Freedom," you read these sentences: "Love is liberating. It offers people both roots and wings." What does this mean? How have you experienced this, and how can you offer it to others?

Living and Loving by the Word

1. I mention 1 Corinthians 12:27 in chapter 12, but let's look at this verse in context:

> The eye cannot say to the hand, "I don't need you!" And the head cannot say to the feet, "I don't need you!" On the contrary, those parts of the body that seem to be weaker are indispensable, and the parts that we think are less honorable we treat with special honor. And the parts that are unpresentable are treated with special modesty, while our presentable parts need no special treatment. But God has put the body together, giving greater honor to the parts that lacked it, so that there should be no division in the body, but that its parts should have equal concern for each other. If one part suffers, every part suffers with it; if one part is honored, every part rejoices with it. Now you are the body of Christ, and each one of you is a part of it.
>
> 1 Corinthians 12:21–27

What does this passage teach you about the importance of appreciating and honoring differences between people?

2. What do the following Scripture verses and passages teach you about how the Holy Spirit works in you to change you?
    • John 16:13
    • 2 Timothy 1:14
    • John 16:8
    • Ephesians 3:16
    • Romans 8:26
    • Galatians 5:22–23
    • 1 Peter 1:2

3. Please read Philippians 2:12–13 (AMPC), which is printed in the section "Turn Yourself Over to God." Who works out what He has put inside of you? Why does He do it?

What Do You Think?

Throughout chapter 12, you read about not trying to change people through human effort, but trusting God to change them. Why do you think this is such a challenge for many people? Is it difficult for you? If so, how can you grow in trusting God to bring about the changes He knows are needed in the people around you?

Take the Love Challenge

Let me challenge you to turn yourself over to God. Tell Him that you know you cannot change yourself, but that you want Him to change you and make you who He wants you to be. Trust Him to do every part of it at just the right time and in creative ways. If you earnestly want what He wants for you, place yourself completely in His hands to make the changes that need to be made, follow where He leads you, and rely on His grace to accomplish something far better than you could ever do for yourself.

Please Accept Me!

Growing in Love

1. According to the first paragraph of chapter 13, as Christians, how do we know that God has accepted us?

2. God accepts us unconditionally, but people don't. Why is it important to learn to deal with rejection?

3. On a scale of 1 to 10, with 1 being "hardly at all" and 10 being "very much," how much do you worry about what other people think of you?

4. Instead of allowing what other people think about you to concern you, whose approval should matter to you?

5. Based on the third paragraph of chapter 13, does someone's rejection of us mean there is something wrong with us? What are some reasons people reject others?

6. Fill in the blanks in this sentence from paragraph 4 of chapter 13:

   "Most people who _____ _____ _____ have been _____ themselves."

7. On a scale of 1 to 10, with 1 being "I really struggle with self-rejection" and 10 being "I love and accept myself completely," how accepting are you of yourself?

8. Do you think you are more gracious, forgiving, and accepting of other people than you are of yourself? Why?

9. Why is accepting yourself so important?

10. Think of someone specific who really seems to need acceptance. In what practical ways can you give them the gift of accepting them just the way they are?

11. Many people are in great emotional pain, often as a result of past rejections that have left them feeling unworthy, ashamed, or unlovable. Do you know anyone who feels this way? How does their pain affect them and their relationships?

12. Just as people can inflict much pain on one another, we can also allow God to use us to bring healing to one another. Consider praying this prayer today: "Lord, I pray that You would pour Your love through me to other people and use me to help them find the healing You desire for them."

13. Is there anyone in your life who is hard to love because of past wounds or rejection, and you find yourself adding to their pain instead of helping to relieve it? How might you change your attitude and approach to this person?

14. Fill in the blanks from this sentence at the end of the section "One of the Best Gifts":

    "Loving someone does not mean that we _____ with all their actions, but it does mean we are _____ and _____ toward them."

15. Much of the hatred in the world today is based on people's refusal to accept differences between themselves and others. What are some of the key differences that seem to be tearing our world apart?

16. Have you witnessed or been part of judgment or criticism among Christians over matters of doctrine or styles of

worship, or for other reasons? Do you think this pleases God? How would sincere love think and act toward fellow believers, regardless of their opinions?

17. Why did God intentionally make all of us different from one another? _____

18. What does "loving from a distance" mean?

19. Is there anyone in your life you feel you have to love from a distance? Why is this best for the relationship, at least for now?

20. Fill in the blanks in this sentence from paragraph 5 of the section "Loving from a Distance":

"You can _____ everyone, but that doesn't necessarily mean that you need to _____ _____ in their presence."

21. Is there anyone you need to love from a distance, but that person wants to be inappropriately involved in your life? How can you take courage from this statement in the section "Loving from a Distance": "Always remember that you have a right to safe relationships"?

22. Fill in the blanks in this sentence from the first paragraph of the section "Love Doesn't Enable Unhealthy Habits":

"Love doesn't always mean _____ of a _____."

This is a simple, but powerful truth. How does it help you in a situation you may be dealing with right now?

23. Do you find yourself habitually enabling someone's bad behavior, rescuing them from the consequences of their choices, or allowing them to take advantage of you? What is the first step toward changing your behavior?

24. Why does it often require more love to discipline someone you care about than to let them do whatever they want to do?

Living and Loving by the Word

1. What do the following verses teach us about the rejection Jesus experienced?
    - Luke 9:22
    - John 7:5
    - Acts 4:10–11
    - John 15:25 (NKJV)
2. Since Jesus encountered rejection, you and I will encounter it also. How do we know this, based on John 15:18–20?
3. Are you waiting to do something better, act better, or somehow be a better person before you accept yourself? What does Romans 5:8 say about this?
4. What can you learn from the story of Jacob, Rachel, and Leah, found in Genesis 29:16–35?
5. In 1 Timothy 1:19–20, why did Paul excommunicate Hymenaeus and Alexander, and how did this show love to everyone involved?

What Do You Think?

Based on your reading of the section "Love Doesn't Enable Unhealthy Habits," what is tough love? What do you think tough love would look like in your relationship with someone who needs it? How do you think it would ultimately be good for them?

Take the Love Challenge

Setting healthy boundaries is a way of loving yourself. It's also a way of loving others, even though they may not like the boundaries. I challenge you to think about the relationships that are difficult for you. How can you love these people while also setting and maintaining healthy boundaries with each one? What specific boundaries do you need to set, and how can you enforce them?

Adapt and Adjust Yourself to Other People

Growing in Love

1. Before reading chapter 14, had the concept of adapting and adjusting yourself to other people ever occurred to you? Why is it a good idea?
2. Without realizing it, have you spent much of your life wanting other people to adapt to you? If so, how has this turned out?
3. On a scale of 1 to 10, with 1 being "rarely" and 10 being "almost all the time," how often do you insist on having your way?
4. Have you experienced dysfunction breeding dysfunction in your life and/or in your family? How have you seen this happen?
5. Do you ever allow people to have their way for the sole purpose of keeping the peace in a relationship? When this happens, how can it get out of balance and cause problems?
6. Why are petty matters not worth arguing over?
7. Consider a circumstance that you don't like but cannot do anything about. Do you continue trying to change it to no avail, or do you trust God to take care of it and remain peaceful?
8. Think about a situation you do not like but cannot change. What adjustments can you make so the situation will be easier for you to deal with?

9. According to paragraph 5 of the section "Adapting to Things," what is the only way to enjoy a peaceful life?

10. Have you ever been through a situation that taught you that God gives grace (power and ability) to handle one day at a time? How did you learn this lesson?

11. Why is it fruitless to try to find grace for tomorrow while we are still living today?

12. Have you reached the point where you can adapt to a situation quickly by refusing to lose your joy over it when you know you cannot change it? When has this happened recently, and how did it make your life better?

13. Do you believe that having peace is more valuable than getting your own way? If so, how did you learn this?

14. When we adapt to people and things in a healthy way, how does our example demonstrate God's love?

15. What is one thing we should *not* adapt to?

16. Why does adapting to people who are different from us require humility?

17. Many divorces and broken relationships take place fundamentally because one or both people refuse to adapt to the other. Have you experienced this or seen this take place? If so, what did it teach you about the importance of being adaptable?

18. What negative emotions sometimes keep you from treating others as you would like to be treated or from doing what Jesus would do in certain situations?

19. Consider a circumstance in your life right now in which you have an opportunity to treat someone else the way you would want to be treated. If you do this, what will it look like? Are you willing to make the sacrifices it will require?

20. If you are accustomed to praying about your needs before praying for other people, I'd like to invite you to make a change. Will you begin to ask God what you can do for Him and for others before you tell Him what you need? Ask Him how you can serve Him and to give you the grace to make any sacrifice needed to show His love to the people around you.

21. In what ways does your busyness keep you from serving others? What can you do to change this?

Living and Loving by the Word

1. How does Romans 12:16 (AMPC) teach us to live?

2. According to Matthew 6:34, what does each day bring and how should we deal with it?

3. In his letters, Paul never prays that people would be problem-free or that their problems would go away. According to Colossians 3:12 (AMPC), how does he pray for them? Why does he pray for them in this way? Is there a specific situation in your life right now that you could stop praying would go away and start praying for peace in the midst of it and for grace to endure it?

4. What lessons can we learn from Philippians 4:12–13? How can you grow in these areas?

5. In 1 Corinthians 9:20–22, Paul writes of adapting and adjusting to others in order to lead them to Christ, but the principles in these verses also apply to ways in which we wish to maintain love, unity, and peace. After reading this passage, what specific ways can you think of to adjust to certain people or situations in your life?

6. How does Matthew 7:12 teach us to treat others? How would this affect our relationships?

7. What lessons can you learn from the parable of the Good Samaritan, found in Luke 10:25–37?

8. What does it mean to be a living letter, or a living epistle, of Christ, as Paul writes about in 2 Corinthians 3:2–3? What kind of letter are you?

What Do You Think?

Were you abused in any way, especially during your formative years? If so, I encourage you to consider that the abuse may have influenced your views on many things and/or the way you behave in relationships. Do you find yourself frequently in conflict with others over the way things should be done and insisting that your way is right? What are these areas? I suggest praying about them, studying what the Bible says about them (you can look them up on the internet using keywords such as "What does the Bible say about raising children?"), and seeking help from godly people who are wise and experienced in them.

Take the Love Challenge

I mentioned that Dave and I feel well balanced in terms of which one of us gets our way in certain circumstances. He gets his way in matters that are important to him, and I get my way in matters that are important to me. Think of a close relationship you have. List some things that are important to the other person and some that are important to you. Do the two of you allow the person to whom each matter is most important to have their way? If some of these points are areas of contention, I challenge you to go to the other person and say something like "I've realized that such-and-such is really important to you, and I want you to have what you want in this area as much and as often as possible." Will you do this?

We Are All Created Equal in God's Eyes

Growing in Love

1. According to the first paragraph of chapter 15, what is the only way to overcome injustice and inequality?

2. In chapter 1 of *Loving People Who Are Hard to Love*, you read: "All prejudice and racial divides would disappear if we all simply loved as God loves." Why is this true?

3. Who falls into the category of "whoever will" and what does this mean, according to the end of the section "God's Universal Call to Whoever Will"?

4. Fill in the blanks from these sentences in the third paragraph of the section "The Racial Divide":

    "Hatred cannot destroy _____, and evil cannot destroy _____. Only _____ can conquer evil, and only _____ can overcome evil."

5. Mahatma Gandhi, who fought injustice powerfully, yet without violence, said: "The weak can never forgive. Forgiveness is the attribute of the strong." Why is forgiveness "the attribute of the strong," not a characteristic of the weak?

6. On a scale of 1 to 10, with 1 being "I don't know anyone who isn't like I am" and 10 being "I have a very diverse group of

friends and colleagues," how inclusive are you? If you have to admit that you are not very inclusive, how can you become more so?

7. Think through the circle of people closest to you. What are some of the ways they represent diversity, and why do you appreciate these things?

8. Technology has made isolation very easy for us. Think about your life over the past several years. Have you become more isolated or less isolated? If you have become more isolated, how can you reverse this?

9. Do you agree that social media has contributed to greater isolation and to greater division among people? How do you discipline yourself and your children (if applicable) regarding the use of social media?

10. What can you do to intentionally break the grip of isolation in your life?

11. Do you tend to avoid people who appear to be different than you are? Or are you friendly to them, communicating the acceptance we all desire and looking for ways to find common ground with them? If avoiding people who are not like you is a weakness for you, how could you become stronger in this area?

12. Will you commit to try to make everyone you interact with on any given day feel better after they encounter you? It doesn't have to be difficult or time-consuming. A simple smile, a quick compliment, a thank-you, or even holding a door open for someone can send an important message of value to people.

13. Do you make an effort to personally help needy people around you or to donate your time, energy, skills, or financial resources to organizations that help the poor?

14. Do you employ anyone in any capacity? Perhaps you are not a business owner, but you hire someone to cut the grass at your house, walk your dog while you're at work, or keep your home clean and tidy. Do you treat these people well and pay them a good wage? Do you need to rethink anything about the way you treat them?

15. Are you guilty of treating anyone with less respect than they deserve as a human being? What can you do on purpose to show this person that you recognize their worth and value?

16. What can you do in the near future to show your appreciation for people who may be undervalued in some area of your life—daycare or church nursery workers, janitors and sanitation workers, mail carriers, bus drivers, retail clerks, and others who help in ways that often go unnoticed?

17. According to the first paragraph of the section "Our Worth Is Not Measured by What We Own," how does God measure our worth, and what does He look at in us? What is most important to Him?

Living and Loving by the Word

1. Even though it was written centuries ago to people in a different culture, how does Galatians 3:28 teach us to think about the inequality that exists in the world today?

2. How can we grow in our understanding that everyone is equal in God's eyes by reading Acts 17:25–28?

3. What did the apostle Peter mean when he said that God is "no respecter of persons" in Acts 10:34 (KJV)?

4. Who does Revelation 22:17 (KJV) refer to when it says "whosoever will"?

5. What does Romans 10:13 (NKJV) teach us about who can be saved?

6. According to 1 John 4:15 (NKJV), who can abide in God and have God abide in them?

7. For whom did God send His Son to die, and who can have everlasting life, based on John 3:16 (NKJV)?

8. What is the only requirement for receiving eternal life (never dying), according to John 11:25–26 (NKJV)?

9. What were God's directions to His people in the Old Testament regarding inclusiveness, according to Leviticus 19:34 and Deuteronomy 10:19? Why does He give these instructions?

10. What do we learn about treating other people well from 1 Peter 4:9?

11. According to Ephesians 2:14, why can we be confident that God will help us when we seek to heal division in relationships?

12. What does James 2:8–9 teach us about the "royal law," meaning love?

13. What can we learn about treating all people equally from James 2:1–4?

14. Fill in the blanks in 1 John 4:20:

    "Whoever claims to _____ _____ yet _____ a brother or sister is a _____.
    For whoever does not _____ their brother and sister, whom they have seen, cannot love _____, whom they have not seen."

15. What are some of the blessings of helping the poor, based on Proverbs 14:31 (NKJV) and Psalm 41:1?

16. Why is Deuteronomy 24:14–15 an important passage of Scripture for people who employ others?

17. According to James 1:27, what is real religion?

What Do You Think?

Please reread this chapter's opening quotation from Martin Luther King Jr. Why do you think hate is too great a burden to bear?

Take the Love Challenge

This chapter's love challenge is simple: Broaden your circle of inclusion. Take an informal inventory of the types of people who are part of your life and ask yourself how you can become more inclusive in your relationships. In addition, think about some people you know who are not part of your close circle of friends and find ways to build stronger relationships with them.

PART 4

God's Love Triumphs over All

"It's Just Too Hard!"

Growing in Love

1. People often say that loving those who are difficult to love is "just too hard." This cannot be true. Why?

2. When you think about loving people who are hard to love, do you say to yourself, "Okay, I can love this person and this person and this person, but there is *no way* I can love *that* person"? Will you open your mind to the fact that if God is calling you to love them, it will *not* be too hard?

3. According to the first paragraph of chapter 16, what makes things too hard for us to do?

4. Why is "It's too hard" an excuse? Why are excuses deceptive?

5. Fill in the blanks in this sentence from the last paragraph of the section "The Deception of Excuses":

    "The devil wants us to stay busy _____ on other people's _____ instead of _____ them, while at the same time being _____ to our own faults, lest we _____ and allow God to change us."

6. According to the second paragraph of the section "What Is Your Excuse?" why do we encounter pressure when we choose to take the narrow path through life?

7. Why is choosing to live for the moment not a good idea?

8. Why do we often do things we know we should not do and then find ourselves surprised by the harvest we reap, meaning the consequences?

9. Chapter 16 specifies four easy ways to love people who are hard to love. What are they?

10. Fill in the blanks in this sentence from the first paragraph of the section "Loving People with Your Thoughts":

    "Our _____ begin a process that our _____ and _____ carry out."

11. Here's a chance to discipline your thoughts toward someone who is hard for you to love. Think of a specific person and list three good qualities about them. Develop the habit of thinking about these qualities, not negative traits, when you think of this person.

12. Are you praying for the people who are difficult for you to love, knowing that someone may find you hard to love?

13. How can you become more merciful in your thoughts toward people?

14. Based on paragraph 4 of the section "Loving People with Your Thoughts," what happens when we are harsh in our opinions and attitudes toward others?

15. What happens to our hearts when we are generous in every way, including showing mercy to others?

16. Fill in the blanks in the second sentence in the section "Loving People with Your Words":

    "Disciplining our words shows spiritual _____, but speaking without thinking about the _____ or possible _____ of our words is _____."

17. Words are powerful. How can you use your words to bring positive power into a relationship that is currently filled with negativity?

18. What do you say about a specific person without thinking, not realizing that your words decrease your joy? What are several things you could say about this person that would increase your joy?

19. Is the idea of loving people with your prayers new to you? Why does it make sense, and why is it powerful?

20. I encourage you to make a list of all the people who irritate you, hurt your feelings, or offend you and who are difficult for you to love. Will you commit to pray for them daily? How will you start?

21. How can you show love to someone who is hard to love with a tangible gift? It doesn't have to be expensive. It could be a cup of coffee, a pastry, or a smoothie for a colleague you find difficult to work with; flowers from your garden for a cranky neighbor; or a magazine that shows an annoying family member that you've noticed their interests and want to support them. Whether it costs a little or a lot, as long as you put thought and care into your gift, it's likely to be meaningful and help soften the person's heart toward you. Ask God to help you choose that special gift.

22. Why is generosity so powerful?

23. Have you ever been the recipient of someone's generosity and experienced the healing and growth it can bring to a relationship? If so, describe the situation.

24. Will you stop thinking it's too hard to love certain people and start saying, "I can do whatever God asks me to do"?

Living and Loving by the Word

1. What does Deuteronomy 30:11 (AMPC) teach us about things that are hard to do?

2. What does Luke 18:27 (NASB) say about things that really are too difficult for people to do?

3. In light of Philippians 4:13 (NKJV) and Philippians 4:13 (AMPC), how should you think about things that are hard?

4. Please read Romans 2:1 and Matthew 7:4. Do you tend to closely examine other people's faults while overlooking your own? Why do people commonly do this?

5. According to Matthew 7:13–14 (AMPC), what are the two choices we have as we go through life? Which one is best? Why?

6. What does the parable Jesus tells in Luke 14:16–20 teach us about how we allow excuses to keep us from experiencing the good that God has prepared for us?

7. Based on the following scriptures, why should we show mercy to others?
   • Luke 6:36
   • Hebrews 4:15–16
   • Jude 2
   • Matthew 5:7

8. What do Paul's teachings in the following scriptures teach you about loving people with your thoughts?
   • 2 Corinthians 10:5 (ESV)
   • Colossians 3:2
   • Philippians 4:8

9. What does Luke 6:27–28 teach us about how we should think about and treat our enemies?

10. Based on the following scriptures, what can people who are generous expect as a result of their generosity?
    - Proverbs 22:9
    - Psalm 41:1
    - Psalm 41:2
    - Luke 6:38
    - Proverbs 19:17
    - Acts 20:35

What Do You Think?

Many people say "It's just too hard" to love certain people. They feel this way for various reasons. Some are afraid of being rejected. Some have tried to love for so long and failed so many times that they feel they simply don't have the energy to try again. Some don't want to invest the time and effort it may take to love someone who is hard to love, even though there are easy ways to do it. What do you think is the biggest reason you personally find it hard to love certain people in your life?

Take the Love Challenge

Hopefully there are not many people in your life who are difficult to love and you can easily choose the one person who is harder for you to love than anyone else. I challenge you to begin right now to love that person with your thoughts, your words, and your prayers. Then, as God leads you, find a way to express love with some sort of tangible gift.

CHAPTER 17

For the Love of God

Growing in Love

1. What is the proof of our love for God?

2. What is the difference between loving people who love us and are easy to love, and loving those who are hard to love?

3. Why is doing something for someone or giving a present to someone and expecting them to reciprocate more like a bribe than a gift or a favor?

4. I invite you to assess the strength of your love for others based on several what-if scenarios:

   • What if you do something for someone and they don't do anything for you? Do you become offended?

   • What if you invite someone to your party, but later they have a party and don't invite you? Do you feel rejected?

   • What if you buy someone an expensive birthday or Christmas gift, and they buy you something very inexpensive that you know they put no effort into choosing for you? Are your feelings hurt?

   • What if they don't buy you a gift at all? Do you resent that?

   Are you willing to keep treating people well simply because it is right and loving—and trust God to take care of you?

5. Why does God expect people who do know Him to do more for others than those who don't know Him?

6. We often pray to be like Jesus. Think about this seriously: How would your life change if you really were like Jesus?

7. God does not require us to allow someone to abuse us, but what does He require us to extend to the people who hurt us?

8. Do you have to like someone or want to be around them in order to love them?

9. Why does our behavior come under scrutiny when people know we are Christians? If you have experienced this, what happened?

10. One person can affect many people in a positive way or in a negative way. How have you witnessed or experienced this?

11. Who has had the greatest influence on your life as a Christian? Why?

12. Think of the people around you. How can you deliberately influence them in positive ways?

13. According to the information in the second paragraph of the section "More Love = More Obedience," what is a good definition and description of biblical obedience?

14. When you listen to a sermon or other Christian teaching, do you make up your mind in advance to take responsibility for what you learn and to obey it, provided that it is godly instruction? Why, or why not?

15. Why do we grow in obedience to God's commands as we grow in the knowledge of His Word and in love for Him?

16. Have you ever done anything that was hard to do based solely on your love for Jesus? Describe it.

17. Think about various ways in which the promise of a reward motivates you. What types of rewards motivate you, and why do they work for you?

18. Describe a situation in which being obedient to God was extremely difficult for you. How did He help you, and how did He reward you?

19. What kinds of blessings have you received as a result of your obedience to God?

20. How can knowing that God has rewards planned for you on earth as well as in heaven change your behavior in the here and now?

Living and Loving by the Word

1. What does John 14:15 teach us about loving God?

2. According to Romans 5:8, how do we know that God does not require us to earn or try to pay for His love in some way?

3. Luke 6:32–36 helps us think about our motives, meaning why we do what we do. What is your motive for loving people, even those who are hard for you to love? What does verse 35 promise us if we truly love our enemies?

4. Please read 1 Peter 2:19–21 (AMPC). How is bearing with undeserved suffering pleasing to God?

5. What do we learn about how to treat others from Matthew 18:21–22 and John 13:34?

6. How does 2 Corinthians 5:20 help us as we think about how to live our lives?

7. Based on James 4:17, what does it mean for us to know what is right to do, yet not do it?

8. In John 21:15–19, what does the word *agape* mean? What does *phileo* mean? By using the word *agape*, what was Jesus helping Peter understand?

9. What do the following scriptures promise to those who are obedient to God?
   - Deuteronomy 28:1
   - Deuteronomy 5:33
   - Joshua 1:8
   - Psalm 128:1
   - Colossians 3:23–24
10. What do we learn about the rewards God has for us from Revelation 22:12 and Matthew 16:27?

What Do You Think?

Obedience to God is not a popular notion in today's world, and many people scoff at His Word. Why do you think this is? How can you live a life of obedience to Him and to His Word in ways that make a positive difference in the lives of the people around you?

Take the Love Challenge

We all have situations in which our flesh simply does not want to obey God. Among other things, we think about how hard it will be, what we would have to sacrifice, how risky it could be, or what it will cost us financially, relationally, physically, or socially. Sometimes we wrestle with these situations for a long time. Are you dealing with something like this right now? I challenge you today to take a leap of faith. Pray and ask God to help you in every way. Then take that first step of obedience to Him.

CHAPTER 18

What in the World Is Going On?

Growing in Love

1. Have you noticed that respect for God's Word seems to be declining rapidly in the days in which we live? Why do you think this is happening?

2. How have you seen a lack of regard for God's Word impact the world at large, your nation, or your everyday life?

3. Fill in the blanks in these sentences from paragraph 4 of chapter 18:

    "What exactly is going on? Why does the _____ seem to be spinning out of control in a _____ direction? We are in the midst of a raging _____ _____ between _____ and _____, and many people are _____ _____."

4. Bad news seems to be coming from every direction, but good things are still happening in the world. What happy or uplifting news have you heard lately?

5. Based on the last sentence of the first section of chapter 18, what are three ways you can be part of spreading positive news?

6. I like to say, "Spend time with unbelievers as long as you are *influencing* them and they are not *infecting* you." In practical ways, what would doing this look like in your life?

7. Have you noticed more Christians being afraid of being mocked or rejected because of their faith? Have you become this way? Pray for Christians everywhere, including yourself, if needed, to stand strong for God, let their lights shine for Him, and allow Him to use them in the world around them.

8. In chapter 18, you read: "Everyone has their own pulpit, even if it is a backyard fence or a desk at work." To have a pulpit doesn't mean being preachy or acting religious; it simply means that we can all find a place to talk about God and His love. Some people make a pulpit out of an exercise machine at the gym or standing in line in a coffee shop. Where's your pulpit?

9. In what ways have you noticed that telling the difference between some people who are Christians and the nonbelievers around them is becoming more and more difficult? Why is this happening?

10. How have you seen the following statement from chapter 18 to be true? "Godly behavior will preach for us if we let it."

11. What does it mean to compromise?

12. Do you know anyone who, because they are deceived, professes to be a Christian, yet lives in ways that clearly violate God's Word? How can you pray for this person?

13. Fill in the blanks in paragraph 8 of the section "The Lines Are Blurred":

> "It is important that we remember that just because most of the people in the world _____ in certain ways, it doesn't make their behavior _____."

We should always choose to follow _____ _____, not the _____."

14. What happens when we choose to live according to God's commands? What happens when we don't?

15. When I preached a message called "Being Godly in an Ungodly World," many people publicly repented for such things as sexual immorality, lying, hatred, jealousy, and other unhealthy behaviors. Is there anything you are doing that you know to be contrary to God's Word? If so, you can take time to repent right now. You can do it privately, just between yourself and God. If you aren't sure how to do it, just say something like "God, I repent for (whatever it is). I ask for and receive Your forgiveness. And I ask You to help me stop doing this and start living according to Your Word." It's that simple, and it's *very* powerful.

16. Have you ever tried to make yourself feel better about some sin in your life by trying to convince yourself that God understands why you do it? He may understand, but sin is still sin. Do you need to reevaluate how you are thinking about any sin in your life and ask God's forgiveness? Why not start today?

17. What is a remnant?

18. Are you willing to sacrifice in order for God to use you to help get this world back on His track?

19. According to paragraph 4 of the section "From Satan's Deception to God's Truth," what is true prosperity?

20. Based on your reading of the section "From Satan's Deception to God's Truth," explain what happened to the authority God delegated to us, and why we can now use it with confidence.

21. What do we believe when we are deceived? Are you praying against deception in your life and in the lives of those around you?

22. What kind of lies have you believed about yourself? What is the truth?

23. What is the only consistent source of truth?

Living and Loving by the Word

1. According to Titus 2:11–12, the opening scriptures of chapter 18, why are many of the problems in the world today unnecessary?

2. How does Romans 1:28–31 describe what you are seeing around you?

3. We do not know for certain whether we are living in the "last days" or not, but what do you see in the following scriptures that describes what is happening today?
   - Mark 13:4–13
   - 2 Timothy 3:1–5
   - Matthew 24:3–12

4. Why is Matthew 24:13–14 encouraging?

5. How do John 17:11–17 and Philippians 2:15 help us learn to be *in* the world, but not *of* the world?

6. Romans 12:2 teaches us not to be conformed to the world, but to be transformed as God's Word renews our minds. What does this mean?

7. How does Psalm 37:1–2 encourage you?

8. What can you believe about yourself, regardless of your past, based on these scriptures?
   - 2 Corinthians 5:17
   - Isaiah 43:18–19
   - Philippians 3:13–14

What Do You Think?

Do you think the world today is in worse shape than you have ever seen it? Why do you believe this has happened? How can you personally make the world a better place? Take some time to think seriously and pray about how you can improve the world in a big way or a small way, knowing that little things can make as much of a difference as big things. Next, make some notes about what you will need in order to do what is on your heart to do. Set a goal for when you plan to accomplish your positive contribution to the world.

Take the Love Challenge

In chapter 18, you read: "If you are going to be a Christian, then be a real one, not just one who goes to church on Sunday and then acts like the world the rest of the week." I challenge you to examine your life and see if there are areas in which you are living more like the world than like a follower of Jesus. Ask God to help you change so you can be more like Jesus and represent Him well in the world.

CHAPTER 19

Love Wins

Growing in Love

1. Why are we as believers called the light of the world, and how can we let our lights shine?
2. According to the third paragraph of chapter 19, how does true love manifest?
3. Fill in the blanks in this sentence from paragraph 4 of chapter 19:

    "When someone does _____ against us and we treat them the same way they treated us, we give the _____ exactly what he is hoping for: _____ and more _____. But, if we _____ evil with _____, we _____ our enemy, Satan."
4. What is the highest and most effective form of spiritual warfare we can wage?
5. Why does God tell us to love our enemies, pray for them, and bless them?
6. What is the antidote to disunity, strife, bitterness, hatred, arguing, anger, and resentment in our lives and relationships?
7. How do our emotions sometimes hinder love?

8. When we choose to obey God's Word instead of making decisions based on our emotions, what kind of progress do we make, and what does it mean?

9. Have you ever chosen to apologize or to say something that was uncomfortable for you in order to obey God's Word and to show love? What happened?

10. What is the difference between feeling your emotions and following them?

11. Have you ever allowed your emotions to keep you from doing something you knew God wanted you to do? If so, how can you prevent that from happening in the future?

12. How can you manage your emotions instead of letting them manage you?

13. Why are people who are filled with darkness not comfortable around Christians?

14. After people are born again, why do they feel uncomfortable doing evil or ungodly things?

15. Are you currently doing anything that would not be considered evil, but for which you feel the conviction of the Holy Spirit and know you should stop it? What is it, and will you commit right now to obey the Spirit's promptings and discontinue it?

16. What is the difference between deliberate, habitual sin and accidental or unintentional sin?

17. What is the only reason we should spend time with unbelievers?

18. Love gives us power, and if we are not walking in love, we are weak and powerless against whom?

19. Fill in the blanks in these statements from the section "Are You Ready for War?":

    "Without love, our _____ are weak."

    "Without love, our _____ is weak."

"Without love, we are _____."

"Without love, we are not _____ God."

"Without love, we open a door for _____ in our lives."

20. Based on your reading of the section "The War Is Spiritual," what is our greatest weapon against the devil? Why?

21. Fill in the blanks in this sentence from paragraph 5 of the section "The War Is Spiritual":

"A believer who _____ God, _____ in love, _____ the Word, and _____ God is _____ to Satan."

22. What is the greatest force on earth, a force that can change the world?

23. How do we know that we have the power to love all people?

Living and Loving by the Word

1. What does John 8:12 teach us about Jesus? If we follow Him, what can we count on?

2. Who are we as believers, according to Matthew 5:14–16, and what are we to do?

3. In Romans 13:12, what does the "armor of light" refer to?

4. According to Romans 12:21, what always overcomes evil?

5. Ephesians 6:10–18 teaches us to put on our spiritual armor. What are the pieces of our armor?

6. James 1:22 (AMPC) says that if we hear God's Word and don't do it, it is because we deceive ourselves through reasoning that is "contrary to the Truth." What does this mean?

7. What do 1 John 2:4 and 3:9 (AMPC) teach us about sin and obedience to God?

8. In practical terms, what does 2 Corinthians 6:14 mean? Have you ever known anyone who ignored this advice and paid a price for doing so?

9. What do 2 Corinthians 10:3–5 and Ephesians 6:10–18 teach us about spiritual warfare?

10. According to Luke 10:19 (AMPC), what has Jesus given us that we must exercise?

11. James 4:7 says, "Submit yourselves, then, to God. Resist the devil, and he will flee from you." But resisting the devil does no good unless we are what? (See James 4:6.)

12. Based on 1 Timothy 1:5 (AMP), what was Paul's primary goal in teaching people?

13. According to Galatians 5:6, how does faith work? Why is this true?

14. Referring to our enemy, the devil, 1 Peter 5:9 says to "be firm in faith [against his onset]" (AMPC). What does this mean?

15. Second Corinthians 10:4 says our spiritual weapons "have divine power to demolish strongholds." What are these strongholds?

16. What does John 3:16 (NASB) teach us about how much God loves the world?

What Do You Think?

After reading chapter 19, I hope you can see clearly that a spiritual war is raging and that our enemy, the devil, seems to be working overtime to sow strife, division, anger, hatred, violence, jealousy, fear, offense, unforgiveness, and causing all kinds of trouble in relationships. One way he works is through negative emotions. What do you think are the primary negative emotions he stirs in you? How does this hinder your ability to love others? How can you defeat the enemy as he works against you in this way?

Take the Love Challenge

You've reached the end of this study guide, and my concluding challenge to you is this: For the rest of your life, love like you've never loved before. Do it on purpose, every chance you get, to everyone you meet.

CONCLUSION

I pray this study has helped you grow in your ability to love everyone, especially people who are hard for you to love. I also pray that you will continue to grow in love each day and find more and more ways to show people you love them.

I hope you will remember several basic truths from this book, because they will help you as you navigate difficult relationships and as you represent Jesus in the world around you. Remember:

1. Love isn't a feeling; it's how you treat people.
2. The way to overcome evil is with good.
3. Without being willing to forgive, it is impossible to love.
4. You don't have to like someone to love someone.
5. God will always help you obey Him, and He wants you to be obedient to Him by loving others as Jesus loves you.

Finally, I'd like to encourage you to reread *Loving People Who Are Hard to Love* any time you find yourself in a difficult relationship. The Holy Spirit may highlight lessons and advice the next time you read it that didn't jump out at you the first time you read it, perhaps exactly the insight you need in a specific circumstance. To further help you, don't forget that there is a section at the end of the book called "Scriptures to Help You Forgive and Find Freedom from Offense."

I hope that through this study, you have gained a fresh commitment to love God, to love yourself by receiving God's love for you, and to love other people any way you can, everywhere you go.

Do you have a real relationship with Jesus?

God loves you! He created you to be a special, unique, one-of-a-kind individual, and He has a specific purpose and plan for your life. And through a personal relationship with your Creator—God—you can discover a way of life that will truly satisfy your soul.

No matter who you are, what you've done, or where you are in your life right now, God's love and grace are greater than your sin—your mistakes. Jesus willingly gave His life so you can receive forgiveness from God and have new life in Him. He's just waiting for you to invite Him to be your Savior and Lord.

If you are ready to commit your life to Jesus and follow Him, all you have to do is ask Him to forgive your sins and give you a fresh start in the life you are meant to live. Begin by praying this prayer...

Lord Jesus, thank You for giving Your life for me and forgiving me of my sins so I can have a personal relationship with You. I am sincerely sorry for the mistakes I've made, and I know I need You to help me live right.

Your Word says in Romans 10:9, "If you declare with your mouth, 'Jesus is Lord,' and believe in your heart that God raised him from the dead, you will be saved" (NIV). I believe You are the Son of God and confess You as my Savior and Lord. Take me just as I am, and work in my heart, making me the person You want me to be. I want to live for You, Jesus, and I am so grateful that You are giving me a fresh start in my new life with You today.

I love You, Jesus!

It's so amazing to know that God loves us so much! He wants to have a deep, intimate relationship with us that grows every day as we spend time with Him in prayer and Bible study. And we want to encourage you in your new life in Christ.

Please visit joycemeyer.org/howtoknowJesus to request Joyce's book *A New Way of Living*, which is our gift to you. We also have other free resources online to help you make progress in pursuing everything God has for you.

Congratulations on your fresh start in your life in Christ! We hope to hear from you soon.

ABOUT THE AUTHOR

Joyce Meyer is one of the world's leading practical Bible teachers. A *New York Times* bestselling author, Joyce's books have helped millions of people find hope and restoration through Jesus Christ. Joyce's program, *Enjoying Everyday Life*, airs around the world on television, radio, and online. Through Joyce Meyer Ministries, Joyce teaches internationally on a number of topics with a particular focus on how the Word of God applies to our everyday lives. Her candid communication style allows her to share openly and practically about her experiences so others can apply what she has learned to their lives.

Joyce has authored more than 135 books, which have been translated into more than 160 languages, and over 37 million of her books have been distributed free of charge worldwide. Bestsellers include *Power Thoughts*; *The Confident Woman*; *Look Great, Feel Great*; *Starting Your Day Right*; *Ending Your Day Right*; *Approval Addiction*; *How to Hear from God*; *Beauty for Ashes*; and *Battlefield of the Mind*.

Joyce's passion to help hurting people is foundational to the vision of Hand of Hope, the missions arm of Joyce Meyer Ministries. Hand of Hope provides millions of meals for the hungry and malnourished, installs freshwater wells in poor and remote areas, provides critical relief after natural disasters, rescues women and children from human trafficking, offers free medical and dental care to thousands through their hospitals and clinics worldwide, and much more—always sharing the love and gospel of Christ.

JOYCE MEYER MINISTRIES
U.S. & FOREIGN OFFICE ADDRESSES

Joyce Meyer Ministries
P.O. Box 655
Fenton, MO 63026
USA
(636) 349-0303

Joyce Meyer Ministries—Canada
P.O. Box 7700
Vancouver, BC V6B 4E2
Canada
(800) 868-1002

Joyce Meyer Ministries—Australia
Locked Bag 77
Mansfield Delivery Centre
Queensland 4122
Australia
(07) 3349 1200

Joyce Meyer Ministries—England
P.O. Box 1549
Windsor SL4 1GT
United Kingdom
01753 831102

Joyce Meyer Ministries—South Africa
P.O. Box 5
Cape Town 8000
South Africa
(27) 21-701-1056

Joyce Meyer Ministries—Francophonie
29 avenue Maurice Chevalier
77330 Ozoir la Ferriere
France

Joyce Meyer Ministries—Germany
Postfach 761001
22060 Hamburg
Germany
+49 (0)40 / 88 88 4 11 11

Joyce Meyer Ministries—Netherlands
Lorenzlaan 14
7002 HB Doetinchem
+31 657 555 9789

Joyce Meyer Ministries—Russia
P.O. Box 789
Moscow 101000
Russia
+7 (495) 727-14-68

OTHER BOOKS BY JOYCE MEYER

JOYCE MEYER SPANISH TITLES

Auténtica y única (Authentically, Uniquely You)
Belleza en lugar de cenizas (Beauty for Ashes)
Buena salud, buena vida (Good Health, Good Life)
Cambia tus palabras, cambia tu vida (Change Your Words, Change Your Life)
El campo de batalla de la mente (Battlefield of the Mind)
Cómo envejecer sin avejentarse (How to Age without Getting Old)
Como formar buenos habitos y romper malos habitos (Making Good Habits, Breaking Bad Habits)
La conexión de la mente (The Mind Connection)
Dios no está enojado contigo (God Is Not Mad at You)
La dosis de aprobación (The Approval Fix)
Efesios: Comentario biblico (Ephesians: Biblical Commentary)
Empezando tu día bien (Starting Your Day Right)
Hágalo con miedo (Do It Afraid)
Hazte un favor a ti mismo…perdona (Do Yourself a Favor…Forgive)
Madre segura de sí misma (The Confident Mom)
Momentos de quietud con Dios (Quiet Times with God Devotional)
Mujer segura de sí misma (The Confident Woman)
No se afane por nada (Be Anxious for Nothing)
Pensamientos de poder (Power Thoughts)
Sanidad para el alma de una mujer (Healing the Soul of a Woman)
Sanidad para el alma de una mujer, devocionario (Healing the Soul of a Woman Devotional)
Santiago: Comentario bíblico (James: Biblical Commentary)
Sobrecarga (Overload)*
Sus batallas son del Señor (Your Battles Belong to the Lord)
Termina bien tu día (Ending Your Day Right)
Tienes que atreverte (I Dare You)
Usted puede comenzar de nuevo (You Can Begin Again)
Viva amando su vida (Living a Life You Love)
Viva valientemente (Living Courageously)
Vive por encima de tus sentimientos (Living beyond Your Feelings)

* Study Guide available for this title

BOOKS BY DAVE MEYER

Life Lines